LEGENDS OF WARFARE

AVIATION

F6F Hellcat

Grumman's Ace Maker in World War II

DAVID DOYLE

SCHIFFER MILITARY
4880 Lower Valley Road ■ Atglen, PA 19310

Designed by Justin Watkinson
Type set in Impact/Minion Pro/Univers LT Std
Front cover photo courtesy of Rich Kolasa.

ISBN: 978-0-7643-5671-1
Printed in China

Published by Schiffer Publishing, Ltd.
4880 Lower Valley Road
Atglen, PA 19310
Phone: (610) 593-1777; Fax: (610) 593-2002
E-mail: Info@schifferbooks.com
www.schifferbooks.com

For our complete selection of fine books on this and related subjects, please visit our website at www.schifferbooks.com. You may also write for a free catalog.

Schiffer Publishing's titles are available at special discounts for bulk purchases for sales promotions or premiums. Special editions, including personalized covers, corporate imprints, and excerpts, can be created in large quantities for special needs. For more information, contact the publisher.

We are always looking for people to write books on new and related subjects. If you have an idea for a book, please contact us at proposals@schifferbooks.com.

Acknowledgments

As with all of my projects, this book would not have been possible without the generous help of many friends. Instrumental to the completion of this book were Tom Kailbourn, Rich Kolasa, Dana Bell, Tracy White, Sean Hert, Scott Taylor, the staff and volunteers at the National Museum of Naval Aviation, Doug Siegfried with the Tailhook Association, and Robert Hanshew with the Naval History and Heritage Command. Most importantly, I am grateful for the help and support of my wife, Denise.

Contents

Introduction

The Grumman Hellcat, by any definition, was a very successful aircraft. Many would argue that it was the best fighter of all time, and back up that claim with an impressive list of statistics.

In two years' time, Hellcat pilots downed 5,223 aircraft and destroyed many more on the ground. While the Corsair is rightfully a celebrated aircraft, the fact remains that three out of every four aircraft downed during World War II by Navy or Marine aircraft were downed by Hellcat pilots. Perhaps even more importantly, only 270 F6Fs were lost in combat, giving the type a whopping 19:1 kill ratio.

Making this all the more impressive is that the Hellcat begun as a "reserve project in case of failure or delay in the Corsair program." Even before Pearl Harbor, the Corsair, produced by Grumman's competitor Vought, had been chosen to replace the Grumman F4F, which at the time of the Japanese attack was the US Navy's frontline fighter. Initially, Grumman's Bill Schwendler and Jake Swirbul worked on improving the firm's F4F Wildcat. Soon enough, it became apparent that there was not enough room in that design to accomplish all that was asked. A new design was needed. That project, designated Design No. G-50, while sharing lines with the F4F, was actually a new design, centered on the 1,700-horsepower Wright R-2600-16 Twin Cyclone engine. The Navy ordered two prototypes of the new design in June 1941.

CHAPTER 1
The XF6F-1

The first prototype of the Grumman F6F was the XF6F-1, originally Grumman Design No. 50, with manufacturer's serial number (MSN) 3188. The Navy ordered this plane under contract number 88263 on June 30, 1941, and upon acceptance assigned it Bureau Number (BuNo) 02981. This prototype had its first flight on June 26, 1942, with Grumman test pilot Robert L. Hall at the controls. *National Archives*

Fabrication of the first prototype was underway when Japanese bombs fell on Pearl Harbor on December 7, 1941. Redoubling their efforts, the first prototype, Bureau of Aeronautics serial number (BuNo) 02981, was completed and first flew on June 26, 1942. At the controls for the twenty-five-minute flight was Grumman's chief engineer and test pilot Robert Leicester "Bob" Hall. While at a glance the gleaming natural-metal-finished F6F fighter looked like the earlier F4F, it was in fact larger, about 20 percent in most dimensions, and substantially heavier.

Like the F4F, the new XF6F would feature Grumman's Sto-Wing. The wing system, designed by LeRoy Grumman himself, allowed the wings to pivot and fold adjacent to the fuselage and with the leading edge parallel to the ground. However, in a departure from previous Grumman designs, which had closely spaced main landing gear that retracted into the fuselage, the F6F landing gear was widely spaced and retracted into the wings.

The initial flight was uneventful, but Hall was not impressed with the performance allowed by the Twin Cyclone. This led to a different engine choice for the second prototype. That aircraft, BuNo 02982, featured a new, larger engine: the Pratt & Whitney Double Wasp SSB2-G (R-2800-10) eighteen-cylinder engine. The R-2800 notably also powered the F4U Corsair and the P-47 Thunderbolt.

The 2,480-pound engine was an air-cooled, supercharged, 2,804.4-cubic-inch-displacement, twin-row eighteen-cylinder radial engine with water injection. With a compression ratio of 6.65:1, the R-2800-10 developed 1,550 horsepower at 2,550 rpm at 21,500 feet and 2,000 horsepower at 2,700 rpm at takeoff. Through a 2:1 gear reduction, the engine was coupled to a three-bladed Hamilton Standard Hydromatic constant-speed propeller with a diameter of 13 feet, 1 inch. The engine itself was 4 feet, 4.50 inches in diameter and 7 feet, 4.47 inches long; weighed 2,480 pounds; and was designed to burn 100-octane gasoline. The second prototype was designated XF6F-3.

The shape of the XF6F-1 shared some obvious similarities with the Grumman F4F Wildcat fighter plane, including the barrel-shaped fuselage, the presence of a turtle deck, and the general shape of the wings. However, the XF6F-1 added substantial bulk to the rather sparse size of the Wildcat. The pitot tube was mounted on a stub mast above the right wing. A noticeable, square-shaped indentation was in the fuselage aft of the side exhausts. The propeller was from Curtiss Electric, and a spinner was mounted on it. *National Archives*

Like the production F6F, the XF6F-1 had a small, fixed window on the fuselage to the rear of the sliding canopy. A wire antenna was rigged between the antenna mast to the rear of the canopy and the stub mast atop the dorsal fin; both these masts were painted in a dark color. *National Archives*

The XF6F-1 is viewed from dead astern. There were six national insignia, consisting of white stars on blue circles: two on the tops of the wings, two on the bottoms of the wings, and one on each side of the fuselage. *National Archives*

The XF6F-1 is observed from the aft left quarter. In tiny lettering on the vertical fin is "NAVY" and the Bureau Number, 02981, while on the rudder is "XF6F-1."
National Archives

In a left-side view of the XF6F-1, the shape of the main landing-gear door is evident. These doors were considerably larger than those of production F6Fs, with a square projection at the front and a rounded one at the rear. As on the production F6Fs, on the side of the fuselage aft of the wing root was a recessed step with a sprung door, and to the side of the cockpit was a recessed handhold, also with a sprung door. *National Archives*

The XF6F-1 had the Grumman-style folding wing, which rotated on two axes, resulting in the wings being folded, leading edges down, alongside the fuselage. *National Archives*

The three-bladed Curtiss Electric propeller and its spinner are seen in this frontal view of the XF6F-1. The prototype was equipped with the Wright Aeronautical Division R-2600-10 Twin Cyclone air-cooled, fourteen-cylinder radial engine, with a displacement of 2,603.737 cubic inches. Details of the wing-fold joint on the outer wing panels are visible. The chin scoop on the cowling had two vertical dividers in it. *National Archives*

The XF6F-1 is viewed from dead astern, with the wings folded. Note the position of the pitot tube on top of the right wing near the wingtip. The tailwheel is turned about 90 degrees to the left and is fitted with a small door on the front of the fork of the tail gear. *National Archives*

The cowling and windscreen of the XF6F-1 are viewed close-up from the right side. Aft of the sliding canopy is a recessed track. A ring sight is visible inside the windscreen, and a corresponding bead sight is on the deck to the right of the photo. The dark-colored spot below the windscreen is a button for releasing the canopy, to slide it to the rear. *National Archives*

The left side of the engine-accessories compartment between the cockpit (*right*) and the engine is depicted. To the lower left are exhausts. To the rear of the compartment is the oil tank, with oval sides and a curved duct above it. *National Archives*

The right side of the engine-accessories compartment is shown, including five exhausts, the oil tank, and ducts.
National Archives

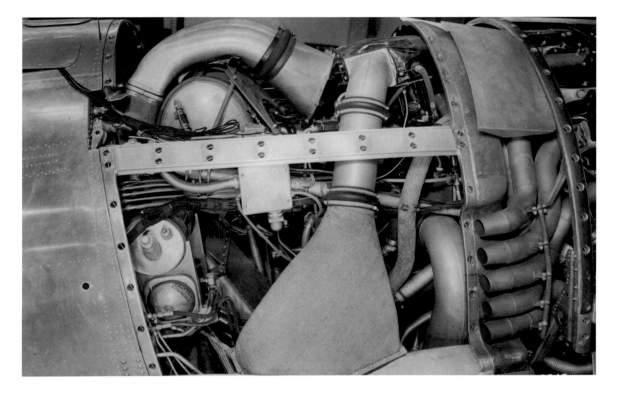

A photo of the right side of the cowling and the forward fuselage of the XF6F-1 provides a clear illustration of the shape of the indentation for the upper cluster of exhausts, as well as the placement of the cowling fasteners. A close view also is offered of parts of the main landing-gear doors.
National Archives

CHAPTER 2
The F6F-3

The first production Hellcat was the F6F-3. It was built to survive a considerable amount of direct hits from machine guns and was powered by the Pratt & Whitney R-2800-10 Double Wasp radial piston engine, rated at 2,000 horsepower. Produced under contract number 90071, the F6F-3 seen in this photo is an early example but is not from the earliest production, since the six machine guns do not have fairings over their muzzle ends. This plane was photographed on October 25, 1943. For extended range, it had an Mk. 2 150-gallon centerline drop tank. It is painted in tricolor camouflage of Sea Blue, Intermediate Blue, and Insignia White. *National Archives*

The R-2800-powered prototype proved to resolve the deficiencies that Bob Hall had noted in the XF6F-1, and was placed into production as the F6F-3. In order to meet the demand for the new aircraft, dubbed the Hellcat, Wildcat and Avenger production was licensed to the Eastern Aircraft Division of General Motors. The Eastern-built versions of the TBF and F4F were designated TBM and FM by the Navy. This move allowed Grumman to devote their Bethpage plant to Hellcat production, but even with that adjustment, the facilities had to be expanded to be able to accommodate the orders. Plant Three was constructed for dedicated F6F manufacture. That plant began operation on June 1, 1942, and the first mass-production F6F-3 rolled out the door on October 4 of the same year—only three weeks after the first F6F-3 airframe flew.

In contrast to the prototype's spinner-equipped Curtiss Electric propeller, the F6F-3 used a full-feathering Hamilton Standard unit with no spinner. Ultimately, 4,402 F6F-3 aircraft were built over a period of nineteen months, ending production in April 1944. Of these, 252 were delivered to the British Fleet Air Arm.

In addition to standard F6F-3 aircraft, eighteen F6F-3E night fighter aircraft were converted from stock F6F-3 aircraft. These F6F-3Es featured Westinghouse AN/APS-4 radar mounted beneath the wing, with its scope in the center of the instrument panel. The cockpits on these aircraft had flat, bulletproof windshields, and inside the cockpit, red lighting was used.

An additional 229 night fighter versions of the F6F-3 were built that utilized the Westinghouse AN/APS-6 radar, which had a radome set into the wing. Designated the F6F-3N, these aircraft were used to offset the loss of Corsair night fighters.

F6F-3, BuNo 04843, the sixty-ninth example of that model produced, is the subject of this series of walk-around photos taken on March 10, 1943. The plane was painted in two-color camouflage of Blue Gray over Light Gray. One of the defining features of very early F6F-3s was the presence of tapered fairings over the parts of the machine gun barrels that protruded from the leading edges of the wings: that feature is visible in this photo. *National Archives*

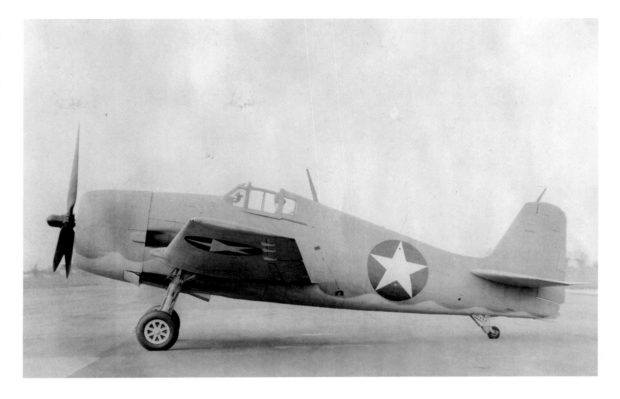

Grumman F6F-3, BuNo 04843, is seen from the left aft quarter. The rudder, elevators, ailerons, and outboard flaps were fabric covered; the balance of the wings, fuselage, and empennage was clad with aluminum alloy. The small fairing that looks like an air scoop on the cowling below the cowl flaps was present on the first 1,500 F6F-3s and then was discontinued. *National Archives*

F6F-3, BuNo 04843, is viewed from astern on March 10, 1943. The wing center section was horizontal; the outer wing panels had 7.5 degrees dihedral. The wings had an incidence of 3 degrees. *National Archives*

The fuselage of the F6F-3 was of stressed-skin, monocoque design. The aluminum-alloy skin had a smooth appearance, with the vertical joints coinciding with the lateral bulkheads and frames. Longitudinal stiffeners made of aluminum-alloy channels and angle running the length of the fuselage gave additional strength to the frame underneath the skin. *National Archives*

In this three-quarter front-right view of F6F-3, BuNo 04843, the small fairing on the side of the cowl, found on early F6F-3s, may be seen. Immediately aft of the fairing is an indentation in the side of the fuselage to provide clearance for a cluster of engine exhausts. A small door is at the front of each main landing-gear (or, in Navy parlance, alighting-gear) bay; doors are also attached to the inboard sides of the main-gear oleo struts. *National Archives*

Several times there were experiments to determine if it was possible to mount an aerial torpedo under the belly of the F6F-3, but evidently Hellcats did not deploy torpedoes operationally. A dummy torpedo has been mounted on F6F-3, BuNo 41588, on March 31, 1945. *National Archives*

The right main landing gear of an F6F-3 is viewed from the forward inboard quarter in a photograph dated February 7, 1943. Two round access doors are open on the bottom of the wing to the front of the main gear. *National Archives*

The right main landing gear is seen from the outboard side on the same plane. The oleo strut, brace, and interiors of the landing-gear doors are painted the same Insignia White as the underside of the wing. In the background are two F4F Wildcat fighter planes. *National Archives*

In a photograph taken on November 11, 1942, the left main landing gear of an F6F-3 is partially retracted. As the gear was swung back toward the wing during retraction, the gear also rotated through a 90-degree arc, so the wheel would lie horizontally in the landing-gear bay. Next to the front of the bay is a jack, which is supporting the plane. *National Archives*

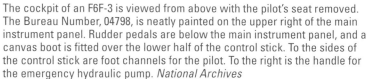

The cockpit of an F6F-3 is viewed from above with the pilot's seat removed. The Bureau Number, 04798, is neatly painted on the upper right of the main instrument panel. Rudder pedals are below the main instrument panel, and a canvas boot is fitted over the lower half of the control stick. To the sides of the control stick are foot channels for the pilot. To the right is the handle for the emergency hydraulic pump. *National Archives*

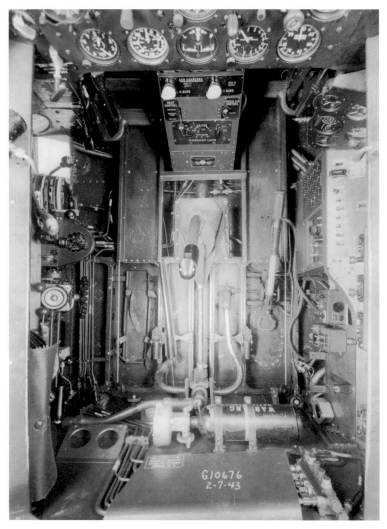

More of the cockpit is viewed from above in a photo dated February 7, 1943. Again, the pilot's seat has been removed. At the bottom is the rear bulkhead of the cockpit, at the center is the control stick, and at the top is the instrument panel. On the rectangular panel below the main instrument panel are controls for the gun chargers, heater, fresh-air ventilation, and fluorescent lights, and a manufacturer's plate with Grumman and US Navy serial numbers and manufacturing date. *National Archives*

More of the control panel below the main instrument panel in a different F6F-3 is shown in a photo dated October 20, 1943. On this panel, the manufacturer's plate is in a higher position, and it identifies this plane as manufacturer's number A-1497 and Navy BuNo 40231. At the top of the panel are the landing-gear emergency control and the wing-folding safety lock control. *National Archives*

In a photo of the left side of the cockpit of F6F-3, BuNo 40231, on October 20, 1943, a checklist is on the canopy sill; on the console are the throttle quadrant and fuel mixture control, wing flap control, controls for cowl flaps and oil cooler and intercooler shutters, and tailwheel lock. Just below the console are the fuel controls, elevator and rudder trim-tab controls, and wing-flap manual control. *National Archives*

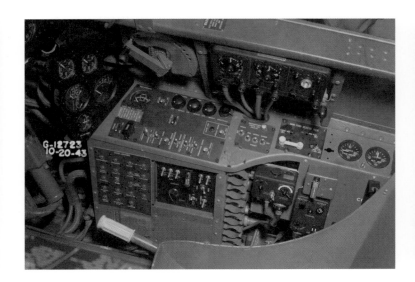

The right side of the cockpit of F6F-3, BuNo 40231, is seen. The canopy hand crank and radio controls are at the top; indicators, gauges, and light controls are on the top of the console; and circuit breakers and controls for armaments and the gunsight are on the side of the console. *National Archives*

For pilot comfort, there was a fold-down armrest on the left side of the cockpit of the F6F-3, and it is shown in its lowered position. *National Archives*

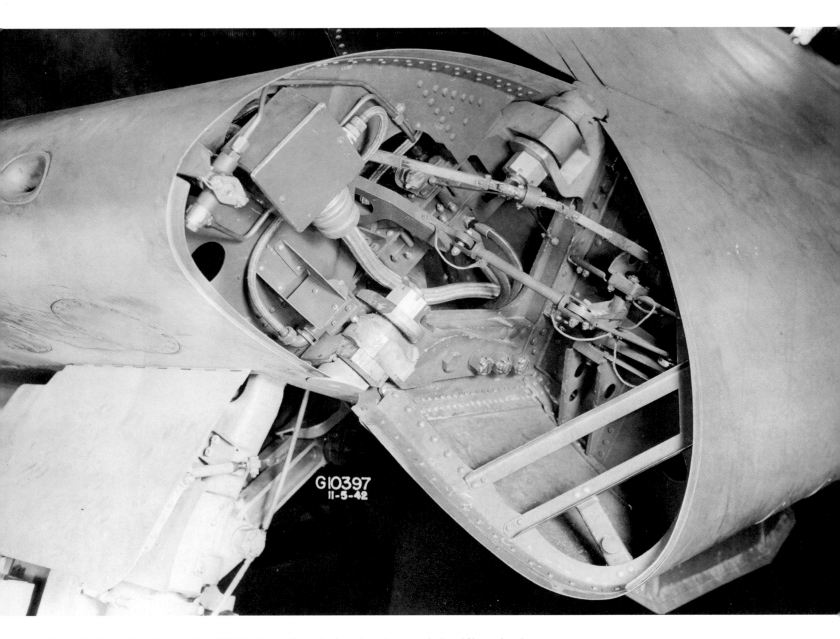

G10397
11-5-42

The fold joint on the left wing of an F6F-3 is viewed from the front in a photograph dated November 5, 1942. To the left is the center wing section, including the upper part of the main landing gear. Note the forward hinge at the top, as well as the various control links, flexible lines, and the two braces on the outer wing section. *National Archives*

The left machine gun and ammunition bays are viewed with their doors open. The guns are staggered in order to gain proper clearances for the ammunition feed chutes. A removable tubular brace is mounted diagonally over the guns. The covers on the receivers of the right and the left guns are open, while the cover of the middle gun is closed. Ammunition boxes are to the top. *National Archives*

The right machine gun and ammunition bays are depicted. Morris heaters are installed on the receivers of these .50-caliber machine guns. No ammunition is installed. Each gun was supplied with 400 rounds of ammunition. *National Archives*

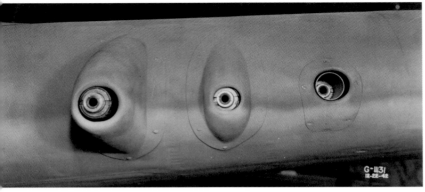

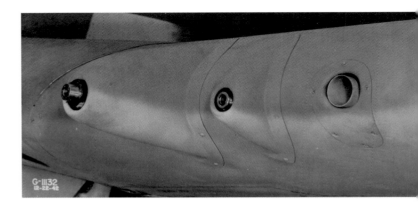

The fairings for the machine guns used on early-production F6F-3s are seen on the left wing in a photograph dated December 22, 1942. The inboard and center fairings jutted from the wing and had teardrop shapes as seen from the front. The outboard fairing was flush with the leading edge of the wing. Inside that aperture, a blast tube extends slightly to the front of the gun muzzle. *National Archives*

The same machine gun fairings are viewed from the left side. The fairings were attached to the wing with screws: slotted roundheaded on the inboard and center fairings, and Phillips flathead screws on the outboard fairing. *National Archives*

In a view of the underside of the right wing of an early-production F6F-3, ejector chutes for the .50-caliber machine guns are on the outboard side of the main landing-gear bay. The larger openings are for spent cartridge cases; the smaller opening to the inboard front of each spent-casing chute was for ejecting links. Also visible is the upper part of the right main landing gear. *National Archives*

The F6F-3 had a gun camera inside the leading edge of the left wing, near the fuselage. Above the camera, on the top of the wing, was a door with a piano hinge on the front of it. That door is shown open here, allowing a view of the top of the body of the gun camera inside. *National Archives*

The aperture of the gun camera is inside the leading edge of the left wing, behind a fairing with a rounded inner edge.
National Archives

The Grumman F6F-3E, of which eighteen were delivered in 1943, consisted of an F6F-3 airframe with a Westinghouse AN/APS-4 radar pod suspended below the right wing. These planes also had identification friend or foe (IFF) sets, red lighting for the cockpit, and radar altimeters. This example, BuNo 41302, was assigned to the Flight Test Division, NATC, at NAS Patuxent, Maryland, and was photographed on May 31, 1944. *National Archives*

The same F6F-3E is viewed from the front. As long as one knows if the airframe was that of an F6F-3, it is easy to determine if a radar-equipped Hellcat was an F6F-3E or an F6F-3N, since the former had its radar pod slung under the right wing, while the latter's radome was faired in to the underside and the leading edge of the right wing. *National Archives*

Grumman F6F-3, BuNo 41930, civil registration number NX30FG, is part of the Friedkin Warbird Collection in Texas. At the time it was photographed, it was in colors and markings of the Fleet Air Arm, portraying a Grumman Hellcat Mk. I and assuming Royal Navy serial number JV188. After World War II, this plane was used as a sprayer and firefighting tanker. In the 1980s it was displayed at the Champlin Fighter Museum. *Rich Kolasa*

Grumman F6F-3 41930, posing as a Grumman Hellcat Mk. I, warms its engine. Black and white invasion stripes are painted on the wings and the fuselage, replicating the identification aid that many Allied aircraft in the European theater wore during the Normandy Invasion in 1944. *Rich Kolasa*

As F6F-3, BuNo 41930, takes off on a flight, the main landing gear is almost retracted into the bays in the wings. This Hellcat lacks the lower cowl flaps: that feature was discontinued on the Hellcats starting with BuNo 39999. *Rich Kolasa*

The same F6F-3 is viewed from another angle as the landing gear is retracting. After these photos were taken, this Hellcat was restored to US Navy colors and markings, receiving a tricolor camouflage paint job. *Rich Kolasa*

Grumman F6F-3, BuNo 66237, construction number A-1257, was ditched in the Pacific during a training flight on January 12, 1944. The Navy recovered the wreckage in October 1970, and for many years it was stored outdoors at the Pima Air & Space Museum, Tucson, Arizona. The Hellcat was restored by Roy Stafford, of Herlong, Florida, and is currently on display at the National Naval Aviation Museum, at Naval Air Station (NAS) Pensacola, Florida. It was painted to match the markings of VF-31 on USS *Cabot* (CVL-28). It should be kept in mind that some of the components and structures on the plane as currently displayed are not original to the airframe as built. *Author*

The Hamilton Standard Hydromatic three-blade, constant-speed propeller of Grumman F6F-3, BuNo 66237, bears decals with the manufacturer's logo and data, including the manufacturer's drawing number, serial number, and maximum and minimum pitch. Behind the propeller is the Pratt & Whitney R-2800 Double Wasp radial engine, below which are the intercooler and oil cooler scoops. *Author*

Grumman F6F-3, BuNo 66237, is viewed from the front right. A Mk. 2 150-gallon drop tank is mounted on the centerline position of the fuselage. The plane is painted in tricolor camouflage: Sea Blue, Intermediate Blue, and Insignia White. *Author*

In a side view of the F6F-3, the tail is painted in the geometric markings assigned in early 1945 to aircraft on USS *Cabot*: white rudder and three horizontal white stripes on the vertical fin. Note the Insignia White countershading below the horizontal stabilizer. *Author*

F6F-3, BuNo 66237, is viewed from the left rear at the National Naval Aviation Museum. Although the camouflage paint on this plane is, of course, a replication of the tricolor camouflage that was directed in Specification SR-2c on January 5, 1943, the original orders called for semigloss Sea Blue on the tops of all airfoil surfaces, and that quality is visible in this paint job. *Author*

The top of the fuselage in the tricolor camouflage scheme was Non-Specular Sea Blue, transitioning lower down to Non-Specular Intermediate Blue. *Author*

The three-white-bar geometric markings on the tail, signifying USS *Cabot*'s air group, are repeated on the ailerons. *Author*

The aircraft number, 17, is marked on each side of the vertical fin, on the fuselage atop each wing, and on each front door of the main landing gear. Fourteen Japanese flags signifying kills, and the nickname "Hawk," are below the windscreen on each side of the fuselage. *Author*

In a photo taken under the right wing of the F6F-3 at the National Naval Aviation Museum, details are available for the right main landing gear and the Mk. 2 150-gallon drop tank. Supporting the tank are two detachable bands and a streamlined fin at the rear. *Author*

In addition to F6F-3, BuNo 66237, the National Naval Aviation Museum owns F6F-3, BuNo 25910. This Hellcat, which crashed in Lake Mission following a landing accident during a carrier qualification flight in January 1945, was recovered in 2009. Prior to its stint as a training plane, this Hellcat had seen combat in the Pacific with VF-38. Restoration of the plane required 15,000 hours of work and was funded by the Taylor Family, owners of Enterprise Rent-A-Car; company founder Jack Taylor had been an F6F pilot on the USS *Enterprise* (CV-6) in World War II. On each wingtip behind a clear, form-fitting lens is a navigation light: green on the right wing and red on the left. Below the right wing, near the wingtip, is the pitot tube. *Author*

The right main landing gear of F6F-3, BuNo 66237, is viewed from the front. A rectangular door with a notch in its upper inboard corner is hinged to the front of the landing-gear bay, while the other, main, door of the bay is attached to the inboard side of the oleo strut. *Author*

The drag links, braces, and bay of the right main landing gear are viewed from below. Toward the rear of the wing, at the bottom of the photo, is the rounded cut in the bottom of the wing, in which the wheel fits when retracted. *Author*

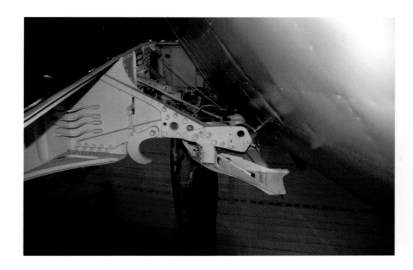

The right main landing-gear bay is viewed from the rear, with the folded outer right wing appearing to the right. In the center is a hook-shaped latch, to hold the oleo strut when the landing gear is retracted. *Author*

The positions of the three staggered .50-caliber machine guns in the left wing of the F6F-3 are depicted. Note the small link rod from the front door of the main landing-gear bay to the upper part of the oleo strut. By means of links, the retraction of the main gear pulled these front doors shut. *Author*

The left landing gear of an F6F-3 is observed from the outboard side, with the folded-down outer left wing visible above. *Author*

F6F Data		
	F6F-3	**F6F-5**
Engine make	Pratt & Whitney	Pratt & Whitney
Engine model	R-2800-10	R-2800-10W
Armament	6 x .50 caliber	6 x .50 caliber or 4 x .50 caliber + 2 x 20 mm
Wingspan	42 ft. 10 in.	42 ft. 10 in.
Length	33 ft. 7 in.	33 ft. 7 in.
Height	13 ft. 1 in.	13 ft. 1 in.
Empty weight	9,207 lbs.	9,283 lbs.
Gross weight	11,381 lbs.	12,598 lbs.
Maximum speed	376 mph	391 mph
Maximum range (miles)	1,090	1,530
Ceiling (ft.)	38,400	37,300

The Steven F. Udvar-Hazy Center, National Air and Space Museum, Chantilly, Virginia, displays this F6F-3 Hellcat, BuNo 41834, which was completed at Grumman's Bethpage, New York, factory in February 1944 under contract NOA-(S)846. The plane was delivered to the Navy on February 7, 1944. At first it served with VF-14, and later it was assigned successively to several other fighter squadrons. After World War II, this plane was used as a manned and unmanned aircraft to gather data on radioactivity after the atomic tests at Bikini Atoll in 1946. This F6F-3 was transferred to the National Air Museum (now the National Air and Space Museum) in 1948. This view from below provides details of the retracted main landing gear, the two pairs of lower exhausts, the wing flaps, the cartridge and link ejector ports, and other features. *Author*

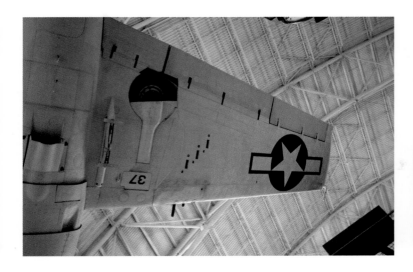

The right wing of F6F-3, BuNo 41834, is seen from below. A bomb rack is installed on this wing inboard of the main landing gear. *Author*

The empennage of Grumman F6F-3, BuNo 66237, is viewed from the right side. The rudder and the elevators were made of fabric over aluminum-alloy frames. The fixed tail surfaces and the trim tabs were of all-metal construction. *Author*

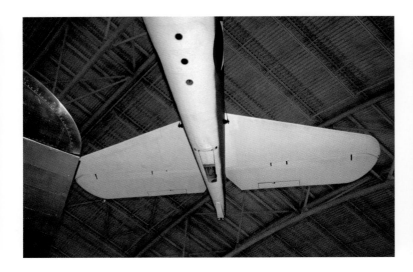

On the bottom of the aft fuselage of F6F-3, BuNo 41834, are three recognition lights: they are, front to rear, red, green, and amber. The tail landing gear has been removed, but the door is in place. Also visible are the horizontal stabilizers and the elevators, equipped with trim tabs. *Author*

The tail landing gear on F6F-3, BuNo 66237, is observed from the right side. Data on tire inflation (115 psi ashore; 160 psi for carrier operations) are stenciled in black on the fuselage. Below the rear of the left bar of the national insignia, above a "LIFT HERE" stencil, is a round opening for passing through a metal bar for attaching a hoist. A similar hole is on the left side of the fuselage, and a metal tube passing across the interior of the fuselage connects the openings. *Author*

The tail landing gear is viewed from the right front. A small, square door is attached to the front of the gear; when the gear is raised, the door seals off the front part of the tail gear bay. *Author*

On the left side of the fuselage of F6F-3, BuNo 25910, which had spent over fifty years underwater, part of the finish of the aluminum-alloy skin and the paint of the national insignia were preserved in the state they were found when the plane was recovered in 2009. This includes the lower half of the star, most of the right bar of the insignia, and part of the left bar. Traces of the red paint on the borders of the insignia are still visible; the red border was authorized for a brief time, from June 28 to September 14, 1943. The red paint seen here likely was covered with blue paint sometime after the blue border was authorized on September 14, 1943. *Author*

The left side of the empennage of F6F-3 BuNo 25910 is portrayed, showing the aft stub mast for the wire antenna; the vertical fin, rudder, and rudder trim tab; and the horizontal stabilizer and elevator. *Author*

The interior of the windscreen and the upper part of the main instrument panel of an F6F-3 is viewed from the right side through the open sliding canopy. Atop the instrument panel is an Mk. 8 gunsight. Behind the windscreen of the F6F-3 was a flat panel of bullet-resistant glass; there was a space between this panel and the windscreen for circulating heated air, for defrosting purposes. Above the Japanese flags on the fuselage is the canopy release button, marked with a white stencil reading, "ENCLOSURE RELEASE." *Author*

Although the plane spent a quarter of a century under the surface of the Pacific Ocean, a reasonably accurate cockpit interior was re-created in F6F-3, BuNo 66237. The red levers below the center of the main instrument panel are the emergency control for the landing gear (*left*) and the wing-fold safety lock control (*right*). *Author*

The main instrument panel and the Mk. 8 gunsight of F6F-3, BuNo 66237, are displayed. The small instrument panel to the lower right of the main instrument panel is missing; this panel included the cylinder-head temperature gauge, oil pressure gauge, oil-in temperature gauge, fuel pressure gauge, and fuel quantity gauges. *Author*

The cockpit of Grumman F6F-3, BuNo 66237, is viewed through the right side of the open canopy. *Author*

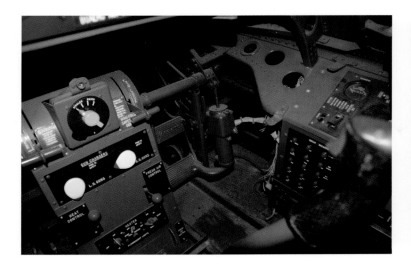

The control panel below the main instrument panel (*left*), the right rudder pedal (*center*), and part of the right console (*right*) are shown. On the top crosspiece of the rudder pedal is the Grumman logo. Circuit breakers are on the side of the console. *Author*

The equipment on the left side of the cockpit of F6F-3, BuNo 66237, appears to be quite complete. According to most reports, Hellcat pilots thought the cockpit was sufficiently roomy, but it tended to be noisy. *Author*

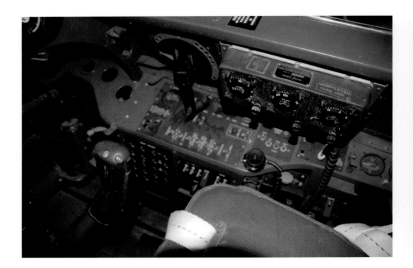

On the upper part of the right side of the cockpit of F6F-3, BuNo 66237, are the hand crank for operating the sliding canopy, and the radio control box (model BC-450-A). To the lower right is the grip of the control stick, which includes a trigger for the machine guns, an intercom switch, and a bomb release button. *Author*

The back of the pilot's head and shoulders were protected by a piece of homogeneous armor plate, with curved indentations on the sides to permit a backward view through the fixed windows behind the sliding canopy. Extending from the bottom of the cushioned headrest is a strip of leather: this was a standard item on some Hellcats. Below the top piece of armor was a homogeneous armor plate to protect the pilot's torso. *Author*

CHAPTER 3

The XF6F-4

Following an August 1942 landing accident, XF6F-1, BuNo 02981, was rebuilt with a single-stage, two-speed supercharger and was designated XF6F-4. This was part of an effort to create a Hellcat suitable for operation from escort carriers. Powered by an R-2800-27, the XF6F-4 first flew on October 1, 1942. The Navy determined that the XF6F-4 did not provide sufficient advantage over the FM-2 Wildcats that were then arming the escort carriers, so the project was abandoned. The XF6F-4 was subsequently reconfigured to utilize four 20 mm autocannons rather than the standard six .50-caliber machine gun armament. While the configuration of four 20 mm cannon was not adopted as standard, these tests did yield data useful later, when some night figures were equipped with one 20 mm autocannon and two .50-caliber machine guns per wing.

The prototype XF6F-1 suffered damage during a landing on August 17, 1942. During repairs, the plane received a new engine with a single-stage, two-speed supercharger, and it was given a new designation: XF6F-4. The engine and engine-accessory compartments of the XF6F-4 are viewed from the right side with their covers removed in a photo dated October 30, 1942. *National Archives*

The cockpit of the XF6F-4 is viewed from above on October 30, 1942. The bottom part of the main instrument panel is at the top, and the mounting frame for the pilot's seat is on the rear bulkhead of the cockpit at the bottom of the photo. *National Archives*

This is a pilot's-eye view of the cockpit of the XF6F-4. The black, cylindrical objects on the sills of the canopy are fluorescent lights for illuminating the instrument panel. Above the rudder pedals are what appear to be foot rests. At the top of the instrument panel is an Mk. 8 illuminated reflector gunsight. For backup, a ring sight is to the right of the Mk. 8 sight. *National Archives*

Parts of the seat belt and harness of the pilot's seat are in view to the left of this image of the left side of the XF6F-4 cockpit. Most of the features are the same as for the F6F-3, with a few exceptions, such as the rotary control for the intercooler and oil cooler shutters on the console just aft of the throttle quadrant, compared to the two small levers for the same purpose on the F6F-3's left console.
National Archives

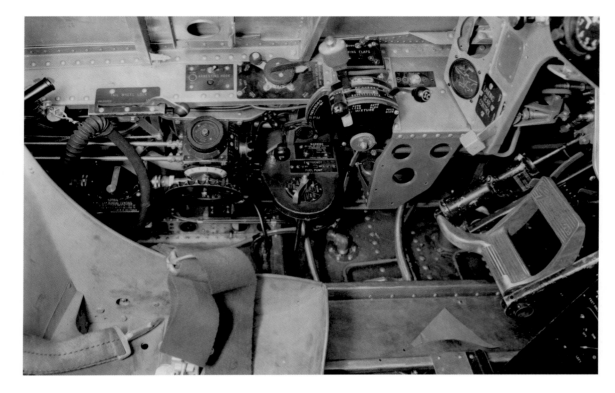

The right side of the cockpit of the XF6F-4 is displayed. The radio controls usually found on the side of the cockpit just below the canopy sill have been moved down to the side of the console, aft of the circuit breakers.
National Archives

In late 1942 and early 1943, experiments were conducted with two 20 mm automatic cannons replacing the three .50-caliber machine guns in each wing of XF6F-4, BuNo 02981. As seen in an overhead view dated March 31, 1943, the outboard cannons were staggered several inches to the rear of the inboard ones. *National Archives*

The XF6F-4 with the so-called cannon wing is seen from the left front. A 150-gallon drop tank is on the centerline position. Note the area of black paint with a curved top, on the fuselage above the wing, where exhaust smudges normally occurred.
National Archives

The XF6F-4 with the cannon wing is observed from the left side. Unfortunately, the Bureau Number on the vertical fin is not legible. Long slots for ejecting spent shell casings are faintly visible on the bottom of the wing.
National Archives

As seen in a March 31, 1943, frontal view of the XF6F-4 with the cannon wing, the outboard cannon barrels appear to be slightly lower than the inboard ones.
National Archives

XF6F-4, BuNo 02981, is viewed from the left rear during 1944, after the four 20 mm cannons had been mounted in the wings. The plane was painted in the standard tricolor camouflage scheme. *Tailhook Association*

The XF6F-4 is displayed with the wings folded in 1944. Tape is wrapped around the muzzles of the 20 mm cannons, and there is considerable wear to the paint on the inboard area of the folded left wing. *Tailhook Association*

The cannon and ammunition bay doors are open on the left outer wing of the XF6F-4 in a photograph dated February 19, 1943. Boxes for the 20 mm ammunition are to the right. The drum-shaped objects on the tops of the receivers of the 20 mm cannons are the ammunition feed units. Note the stiffener ribs on the inner side of the cannon bay door. *National Archives*

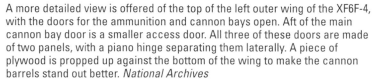

A more detailed view is offered of the top of the left outer wing of the XF6F-4, with the doors for the ammunition and cannon bays open. Aft of the main cannon bay door is a smaller access door. All three of these doors are made of two panels, with a piano hinge separating them laterally. A piece of plywood is propped up against the bottom of the wing to make the cannon barrels stand out better. *National Archives*

The left outer wing of the XF6F-4 is seen in its folded position, with the cannon and ammunition access doors open. Each of the doors is equipped with a hold-open brace. *National Archives*

CHAPTER 4
The XF6F-2

Grumman XF6F-2, BuNo 66244, was an experiment to mate a Birmann model P14B turbosupercharger with two different radial engines in a Hellcat airframe: first, the Wright R-2600-15, and then the Pratt & Whitney R-2800-21 Double Wasp. Although one might conclude that the XF6F-2 came close on the heels of the XF6F-1, it actually was produced after F6F-5 production had begun. The first flight of the XF6F-2 was on January 7, 1944; the pilot was Carl Alber. This photo and the following sequence of walk-around views taken outdoors date to February 7, 1944. The nickname "Fuzzy Wuzzy" is faintly visible on the cowling, a reference to the many small felt-tuft airflow indicators affixed to the fuselage. *National Archives*

The XF6F-2 is viewed from the front right. The cowling was modified with a deeper bottom and taller chin scoop than on production Hellcats. *National Archives*

G-14101
2-7-44

The purpose of the light-colored material on the sides of the fuselage at the time these photos were taken is unclear, but it appears from close examination to have been a thin material that was laid over the fuselage skin. The material partially covered the "TEST" markings on the fuselage sides. *National Archives*

The XF6F-2 is seen from dead astern. The wider stance of the landing gear was one of the key improvements over the Grumman F4F Wildcat. *National Archives*

The XF6F-2 is viewed from astern on February 7, 1944, one month after its first flight. The Navy hoped that the Birmann P14B turbosupercharger would give the Hellcat much additional power at high altitude, and it did make possible sea-level speeds at 20,000 feet of altitude, but the Birmann in the XF6F-2 proved to be a hazard, sometimes causing fires when the hot engine exhausts ignited unburned fuel emitted from the turbosupercharger. Largely for this reason, the Navy declined to adopt the Birmann P14B for the Hellcat. *National Archives*

On each side of the lower part of the redesigned cowling, below and to the front of the leading edge of the wing of the XF6F-2 was an exit vent. Also, there was an air scoop toward the rear of the bottom of the cowling. *National Archives*

Both the redesigned cowling with the deeper chin scoop and the semicircular air scoop on the bottom of the cowling are visible in this frontal view of the XF6F-2. The felt airflow indicators are visible as black splotches on the bottom of the cowling. *National Archives*

The second engine tested in the XF6F-2, the Pratt & Whitney R-2800-21, is seen installed on that aircraft on October 17, 1943. The Pratt & Whitney logo plate, featuring a flying eagle, is faintly visible on the bottom of the reduction-gear enclosure, just behind the front of the propeller shaft. Behind the center of the chin scoop is the oil cooler, to each side of which are the intercoolers. *National Archives*

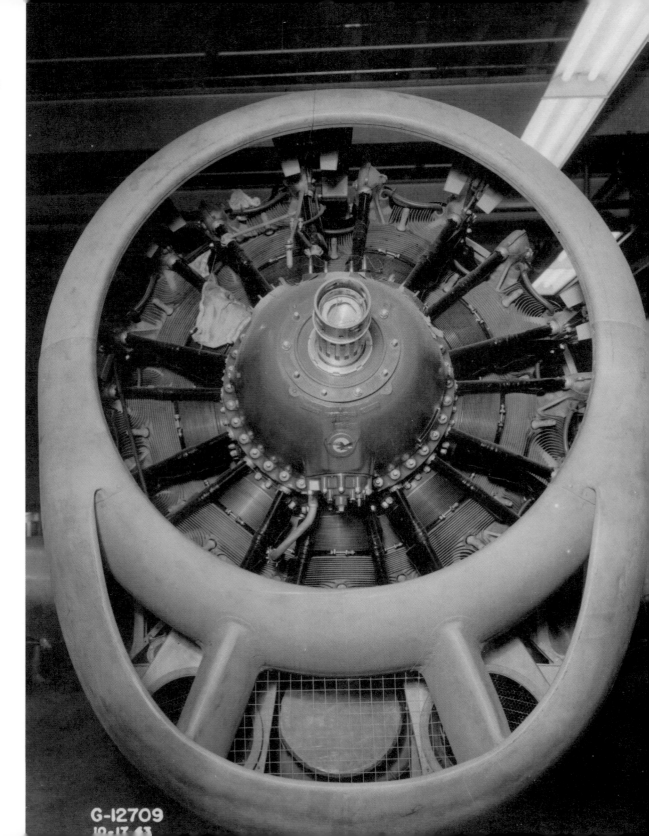

G-12709
10-17-43

The left side of the engine compartment and the engine-accessory compartment are visible with the cowling panels removed. The engine is the Pratt & Whitney R-2800-21, below which are the intercoolers and the oil cooler. To the lower rear of the engine, and inboard of the large, vertical exhaust duct, the bottom of the Birmann P14B turbosupercharger is in view. *National Archives*

The engine and engine-accessory compartments are viewed from the right side with the cowling panels removed on October 17, 1943. *National Archives*

The same components seen in the preceding photo are observed from farther away and farther aft. The outer wing has been removed, as has the engine oil tank. *National Archives*

This photo was taken to document the oil line installation on the lower left quarter of the engine-accessory compartment of the XF6F-2 on October 17, 1943. *National Archives*

The cockpit of the XF6F-2 is seen in a photograph from February 4, 1944. The main instrument panel seems to be the same one used in the F6F-3, but the smaller instrument panel between the rudder panels was different than that in the F6F-3, with more gauges. *National Archives*

The right side of the cockpit of the XF6F-2 was essentially identical to that of the production F6F-3, with canopy hand crank and radio controls at the top; voltameter, pitot tube and battery on/off switches, arrestor hook control and indicator, and light switches on top of the console; circuit breakers and gunsight controls on the side of the console; and a hydraulic hand-pump handle next to the seat. *National Archives*

The left side of the XF6F-2 cockpit was nearly identical to that of the cockpit of the F6F-3, except the former had an intercooler control just below the black-colored checklist placard on the canopy sill. Some of the features are, *right to left*, the landing-gear control, throttle quadrant and fuel mixture control, fuel tank selector control (below rear of throttle quadrant), cowl-flaps control, rudder trim tab control, and tailwheel lock control. After being tested and then rejected for further development, the XF6F-2 was converted to F6F-3 standards. *National Archives*

CHAPTER 5
The F6F-5

The second principal model of Hellcat, the F6F-5, was in production from April 1944 to November 1945. Improvements over the F6F-3 model included an upgrade in the power plant to the Pratt & Whitney R-2800-10W engines with water injection, spring tabs on the ailerons for better maneuverability and combat efficiency, a redesigned windscreen, extra armor, and a slightly redesigned cowling that fit more tightly around the engine. This photo, dated December 29, 1944, depicts an F6F-5 armed with six 5-inch high-velocity aircraft rockets (HVAR) under the wings and two Tiny Tim rockets under the fuselage. *National Museum of Naval Aviation*

The F6F-5 followed the F6F-3 in pouring from the production line in April 1944. The F6F-3 design had few flaws, and the F6F-5 differed little from it. So little, in fact, that absent being able to verify the Bureau Number painted on the tail, the surest means of distinguishing the two models during World War II was by the paint scheme. Coincidentally, the Navy mandate to adopt an overall gloss Sea Blue paint scheme in lieu of the tricolor camouflage scheme coincided with the Grumman changeover from F6F-3 production to F6F-5 production. The F6F-3 Hellcats were finished in tricolor, while the F6F-5 wore blue all over. Internally, the F6F-5 used the same Pratt & Whitney R-2800-10W water-injected engine as did the late F6F-3 models. However, an additional thirty pounds of armor beefed up the pilot's protection to above that provided for the F6F-3 pilot. The addition of six zero-length launch stubs for rockets and Mk. 51 bomb racks beneath the wings further increased the Hellcat's ground attack capabilities.

In addition to the standard fighter, Grumman produced 1,434 F6F-5N night fighters. The F6F-5N utilized the same AN/APS-6 radar as had the F6F-3N. It was equipped with a GR-1 autopilot and flame-dampening exhaust stacks. Some of these aircraft were equipped with an armament suite including two AN-M2 20 mm autocannons and four .50-caliber machine guns.

A further variant was the F6F-5P, a photoreconnaissance Hellcat. These aircraft were equipped to carry a K-19 aerial camera just aft of the port wing trailing edge, and a second such camera in the belly. Typically, one aircraft in each Hellcat squadron was an F6F-5P. Armament and performance was the same as that of a standard F6F-5.

Grumman built a total of 7,870 F6F-5 aircraft, including an impressive 664 delivered in a single month—March 1945. The British Fleet Air Arm received 850 standard F6F-5s, designating them Hellcat Mk. IIs, except for the eighty F6F-5Ns, which the British designated Hellcat NF Mk. IIs. Each Hellcat cost the US government $35,000, substantially less that the $53,000 cost of a Vought Corsair.

After World War II, the Navy modified some aircraft to F6F-5K configurations. These could be used as drones or drone controllers or could be flown normally. These were used either in training units or in combat as flying bombs. In fact, the last US Navy combat operation with a Hellcat was during the Korean War, when pilotless Hellcat drones were launched from USS *Boxer*. Six successful attacks were made by the pilotless aircraft, each carrying a 1,000-pound bomb.

Grumman F6F-5, BuNo 58310, is parked with wings folded during evaluations at NAS Patuxent River, Maryland, on June 1, 1944. This was the 311th F6F-5; the first one bore BuNo 58000. The plane is painted in the overall glossy Dark Sea Blue camouflage that the US Navy directed for fighter planes in Amendment 1 to SR-2d on March 13, 1944; this paint scheme was the rule for F6F-5s. *National Archives*

The last three digits of the Bureau Number of F6F-5, 72731, are painted in large figures on the cowling, in a view taken at NAS Patuxent River on February 1, 1945. Zero-length stub launchers for three HVARs are visible under the wing. The small, fixed windows aft of the sliding canopy on each side of the plane, present throughout F6F-3 and early F6F-5 production, were deleted somewhere between the 1,000th and the 1,500th F6F-5. *National Archives*

F6F-5, BuNo 72731, is observed from the left rear quarter at NAS Patuxent River on February 1, 1945. Visible at the center of the left aileron is the spring tab, a new feature on the F6F-5s. The tabs on both ailerons had an automatic feature, and the left tab also could be controlled by the pilot. A fixed tab, not easily discerned in this photo, also was on the trailing edge of each aileron, inboard of the spring tab. *National Archives*

From this angle, the fixed tab on the left aileron of F6F-5, BuNo 41588, is visible. Early F6F-5s such as this example retained the two fixed windows aft of the sliding canopy. A bomb weighing up to 1,000 pounds could be mounted on a pylon on the belly to each side of the centerline. A 150-gallon drop tank is mounted in the centerline position. The photo is dated March 2, 1945. *National Archives*

A very late (the seventy-eighth from last) F6F-5, BuNo 94443, Naval Air Test Center (NATC), is parked on a hardstand on December 13, 1949. The plane has markings on its tail for the NATC at NAS Patuxent River, Maryland. The white bars on the national insignia have the red bars authorized during 1947. *National Archives*

Grumman delivered a small number of F6F-5E night fighters. Similar to the F6F-3E, the F6F-5E had an AN/APS-4 radar pod under the right wing. This example was BuNo 70678. The AN/APS-4 pod is mounted on a block-shaped pylon, with a sway brace on each side. *National Archives*

Approximately 1,459 F6F-5N night fighters were delivered with AN/APS-6 radar equipment, including a radome pod on the right wing similar to that carried on the F6F-3N. Many F6F-5Ns were armed with two 20 mm cannons and two .50-caliber machine guns. This suite of guns is present on this F6F-5N, BuNo 79139, which also is fitted with a searchlight pod on the left wing. The photo was taken at NAS Patuxent River on August 29, 1945. *National Archives*

Grumman F6F-5N, BuNo 79139, is seen from the right side at NAS Patuxent River on August 29, 1945. Below the cockpit is marked "ASDEVLANT," the acronym for Antisubmarine Development Detachment, Atlantic Fleet, whose headquarters were at NAS Quonset Point, Rhode Island. *National Archives*

The same F6F-5N is viewed from head-on. Three zero-length launchers for HVARs are visible on the bottom of each wing. The outboard machine gun apertures on the leading edges of the wings are taped over, since no guns are installed in those positions. *National Archives*

In August 1945, an F6F-5N bearing the number "4" on the tail is flying over NAS Quonset Point, Rhode Island. The landing-gear doors were painted a light color, likely white, and the plane had the configuration with two 20 mm cannons and two .50-caliber machine guns. Note how the white bar of the national insignia on the bottom of the wing wraps around the radome. *National Archives*

The instrument panel of an F6F-5N is displayed during the battle for Peleliu, on September 25, 1944. The hand is pointing to the radar scope. On the bottom right of the instrument panel is a label giving the plane's Bureau Number: it appears to be 58801. Marine Night Fighting Squadron 541 (VMF N-541), equipped with F6F-5Ns, served in the battle for Peleliu. *National Archives*

The Flying Heritage & Combat Armor Museum, Everett, Washington, owns this airworthy Grumman F6F-5 Hellcat, civil registration number NX79863. The airframe was constructed as a night fighter version, but the plane never saw combat. After World War II, it was converted to a remote-controlled drone and was carried on the US Navy inventories until 1961. *Tracy White*

The Flying Heritage & Combat Armor Museum's F6F-5 is seen from the front right during a flight.
Tracy White

The F6F-5 is finished in markings characteristic of fighter aircraft assigned to USS *Randolph* (CV-15) during World War II: white tail with three stripes of the plane's Glossy Dark Sea Blue, and white ailerons.
Tracy White

The F6F-5 now owned by the Flying Heritage & Combat Armor Museum has been featured at numerous air shows since the 1970s, participated in Grumman's fiftieth anniversary in 1980, and flew across the Atlantic by way of Iceland in the 1990s. *Tracy White*

The same plane is viewed from the left front at an airfield. The current civil registration number is painted in white below the horizontal stabilizer. *Tracy White*

Grumman F6F-5 Hellcat, civil registration number NX79863, is seen in its indoor display setting at the Flying Heritage & Combat Armor Museum, Everett, Washington. *Tracy White*

Some of the cowling and engine-accessory compartment panels have been removed, enabling a view of interior components. In the compartment to the upper rear, the engine oil tank and the engine support may be seen. In the lower part of the engine compartment, below the exhausts, is a supercharger air intake duct. *Tracy White*

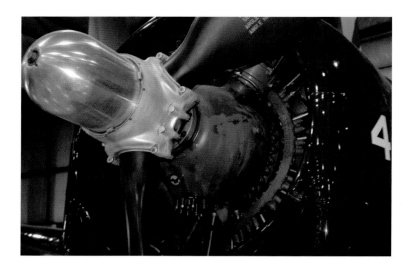

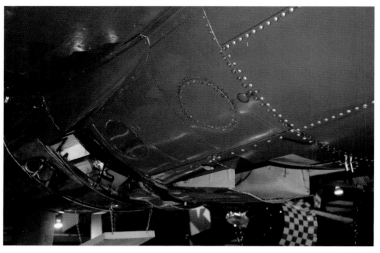

The Air Zoo Aerospace & Science Museum, in Kalamazoo, Michigan, maintains an F6F-5 with manufacturer's construction number A-10828 and BuNo 79683. This photo focuses on the hub and dome of the Hamilton Standard Hydromatic constant-speed propeller and the bowl-shaped reduction-gear housing on the front of the Pratt & Whitney R-2800 engine. *Author*

The belly of the Air Zoo's F6F-5 is viewed from the left side, with the cowling to the lower left and the fillet at the wing root above it. *Author*

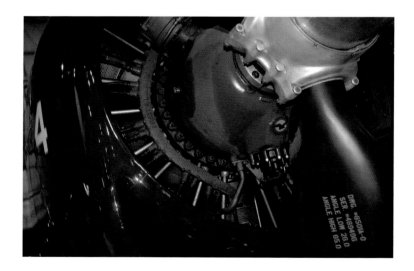

A close-up view of the engine of the Air Zoo's F6F-5 shows the small, blue Pratt & Whitney logo plate on the lower front face of the gear-reduction housing, and the right distributor projecting from the upper part of that housing. Also in view are some of the push rods and the ignition harness. Note the yellow data stencil on the propeller blade. *Author*

The three .50-caliber machine gun barrels in the right wing are displayed. Note the removable fairings the barrels protrude through; they are engineered to match the contours of the leading edge of the wing. *Author*

The Air Zoo's F6F-5 has Goodyear-made solid-spoked wheels for the main landing gear, as opposed to the open-spoked type. *Author*

The right main landing gear is seen from the right rear. The brake line is retained by several metal ferrules attached to the strut. *Author*

The left main landing gear is observed from aft, including a view up into the gear bay. At the top center is the hook that locked the gear in place when retracted into the wing. *Author*

The mechanisms at the top of the left main landing gear of the Air Zoo's Hellcat are viewed from the inboard side of the gear. At the top center is the bare-metal left hook for the catapult bridle. At the bottom is the top of the landing-gear door. To the front of the oleo strut is the small front door for the landing gear. *Author*

The tail landing gear of the Air Zoo's F6F-5 is seen from the left side. *Author*

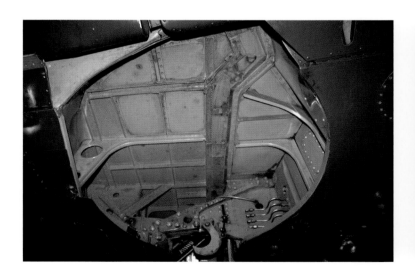

The rear of the left main landing-gear bay is viewed, looking forward. Running fore and aft to the right of the center of the top of the bay is the wing-fold joint. *Author*

The right elevator is slightly raised, allowing a view of the rear face of the horizontal stabilizer. That face is perforated with a series of lightening holes. *Author*

CHAPTER 6
The XF6F-6

The final, and fastest, Hellcat was the XF6F-6. In 1944, two incomplete F6F-5 airframes, BuNos 70188 and 70913, were diverted to create two prototypes of an even-better Hellcat. These aircraft were equipped with 2,100-horsepower R-2800-18W water-injected engines and turning Hamilton Standard four-blade propellers and were designated XF6F-6.

Grumman test pilot Pat Gallo made the first flight in an XF6F-6 on August 30, 1944, and pushed the new Grumman 'cat to 425 miles per hour. Grumman proposed to put the new model in production the following month. However, another new Grumman fighter had also first flown in August—the XF8F-1 Bearcat. The Bearcat had surpassed both the XF6F-6 and the F4U-4 in maximum speed and promised even-greater performance. Rather than introduce a new model of the Hellcat, with an apparently short production run, and further complicate the supply and support chain, the Navy directed Grumman to continue building the F6F-5 until the F8F entered production in 1945.

Two examples of the XF6F-6, BuNo 70913 (shown here) and BuNo 70188, were up-engined conversions of unfinished F6F-5 airframes, with R-2800-18W engines rated at 2,100 horsepower and four-bladed Hamilton Standard propellers. The first flight for an XF6F-6 was on July 16, 1944, with the plane performing at 417 miles per hour at 21,700 feet. Initially, the Navy planned to commence production of the F6F-6 in September 1944, but it canceled these plans in favor of starting production of the Grumman F8F-1 Bearcat. *Tailhook Association*

XF6F-6, BuNo 70913, is seen from the right side at the Naval Aviation Test Center, NAS Patuxent River, Maryland, on December 20, 1944. *Tailhook Association*

A final photo of XF6F-6, BuNo 70913, at NAS Patuxent River on December 20, 1944, captures the aircraft from the left rear. *Tailhook Association*

CHAPTER 7

Combat

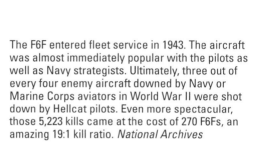

The F6F entered fleet service in 1943. The aircraft was almost immediately popular with the pilots as well as Navy strategists. Ultimately, three out of every four enemy aircraft downed by Navy or Marine Corps aviators in World War II were shot down by Hellcat pilots. Even more spectacular, those 5,223 kills came at the cost of 270 F6Fs, an amazing 19:1 kill ratio. *National Archives*

In January 1943, VF-9 was equipped with the F6F-3, becoming the first Hellcat squadron. This squadron, along with VF-5, became the first squadrons to use the Hellcats in combat as well, flying into battle on August 31, 1943, in an attack on Marcus Island. On November 23–24, Hellcats tangled with Japanese Zeros over Tarawa, with the Hellcats claiming thirty downed Mitsubishis while sustaining the loss of just one of their own. As part of that action, twelve F6F-3 from VF-16 engaged a force of twenty-one to twenty-three fighters, downing seventeen Japanese aircraft, with two more probable. All twelve VF-16 Hellcats returned safely to USS *Lexington*.

While the Zero was more maneuverable than the Hellcat, the big Grumman was simply more powerful. The massive Pratt & Whitney meant that the Hellcat could overtake and outrun the Zero. Combined with the heavy punch of the six big fifties and the rugged construction of the F6F, Allied pilots could control the battle.

The Hellcat was so dominant that 305 Hellcat pilots obtained ace status. Included in this was Capt. David McCampbell, the Navy's all-time leading ace, who scored all thirty-four of his kills while flying the Hellcat.

In addition to air-to-air combat, F6Fs dropped over 6,500 tons of bombs on enemy targets. Further, the big fighter was simple, rugged, and easy to maintain, with some sources estimating greater than 90 percent availability in combat squadrons.

In the Atlantic, British Fleet Air Arm pilots flying Hellcats downed two German Messerschmitt Bf 109s and a Focke-Wulf Fw 190.

Despite a victory ratio almost twice that of the Corsair, following World War II the bulk of the Hellcats was quickly relegated to storage, scrapped, or transferred to training reserve squadrons. The exception to this was the F6F-5N, which remained in fleet service until the last were retired by VC-4 in September 1953.

This Grumman F6F-3 flying at low speed with wheels down near NAS Alameda, California, is evidently the same Hellcat with the F-36 side number in the preceding photo. Details of exhaust and oil stains and paint wear seem to be the same on both planes. The aircraft's number is 36, marked on the fuselage, wing, and cowling. A label attached to the photo states that this Hellcat was assigned to VF-4 and that the image was taken on May 15, 1943. *National Museum of Naval Aviation*

Two very early Grumman F6F-3s are flying over San Francisco Bay, California, in or around mid-May 1943, with the San Francisco–Oakland Bay Bridge, Yerba Buena Island, and man-made Treasure Island below them and the city of San Francisco in the background. The plane to the rear is unmarked, but the closer one has a partial side number: F-36. On April 29, 1943, the Pacific Fleet had ordered the omission of the squadron number, formerly marked at the beginning of the side number. Both planes are among the approximately first sixty F6F-3s issued with the Non-Specular Blue Gray over Light Gray camouflage scheme and national insignia on the tops and bottoms of both wings. *National Archives*

Very early F6F-3 Hellcats with wings folded, assigned to VF-9, are in the foreground on the flight deck of
USS *Essex* (CV-9) during the carrier's shakedown cruise on March 20, 1943. Farther to the rear are
Douglas SBD-4 Dauntlesses from Carrier Air Group 5. Fighting Squadron 9 was the first squadron to be
equipped with Hellcats, in mid-January 1943. These planes have the Blue Gray over Light Gray
camouflage and still have the national insignia on the tops of the right wings, a feature discontinued after
January 1943. *National Archives*

Aviation Mechanic's Mate 3rd Class Julian J. Bik, *left*, and Aviation Mechanic's Mate 2nd Class Elwayn R. Burger, *right*, are lifting cowling panels from an F6F-3, aircraft number 65, exposing to view the Pratt and Whitney R-2800-10 Double Wasp engine and some of the exhausts. The zinc chromate primer on the interior of the panels and on the cowling frame is of a predominantly yellow tint. *National Archives*

Grumman F6F-3 Hellcats from VF-1 are being embarked aboard USS *Yorktown* (CV-10) at Norfolk Naval Base, Virginia, in preparation for the carrier's shakedown cruise to Trinidad, British West Indies, in May 1943. *National Archives*

Sailors on the superstructure watch as the launch officer, called "Fly One," on the flight deck toward the left, drops the flag to signal the pilot of an F6F-3 Hellcat from VF-1 to take off from USS *Yorktown* (CV-10). This was during that *Essex*-class carrier's shakedown cruise in late May 1943. The Hellcat is a very early F6F-3, with tapered fairings over the machine gun barrels and the Non-Specular Blue Gray over Light Gray camouflage. *National Archives*

In another photo taken in late May 1943 during USS *Yorktown*'s shakedown cruise, two airedales lying underneath the wings of an early F6F-3 are about to remove the chocks from the wheels, preparatory to the plane's takeoff. The aircraft number, 4, is on the landing-gear door. *National Archives*

The pilot of an F6F-3 waits for Fly One (*left*) to drop his checkered flag as the signal to take off, on the flight deck of USS *Yorktown* (CV-10). The plane's number, 22, is visible on the fuselage below the left horizontal stabilizer. This photograph appears to be related to a series of color photos taken on the *Yorktown* in or around October 1943. The diagonal white stripe on the tail was a recognition aid for the *Yorktown*'s air group. *Naval History and Heritage Command*

In a photo likely taken in the late summer or early fall of 1943, two F6F-3 Hellcats are preparing to move forward into takeoff position on USS *Yorktown*. The plane to the right has the red border around the national insignia, while a close examination of the plane to the left seems to indicate the insignia under the right wing is the type introduced in mid-August 1943, with a blue border around the white side bars. *Naval History and Heritage Command*

In the foreground on the flight deck of USS *Yorktown* in May 1943, F6F-3 Hellcats are warming their engines, while in the last several rows, Curtiss SB2C Helldivers are doing the same. Between the Hellcats and Helldivers, numerous Avengers prepare to take off. *National Archives*

Plane handlers on USS *Yorktown* are pushing an F6F-3, plane number 11, to its spot on the flight deck during May 1943. A wheel chock is lying on the center wing section to the left side of the fuselage. *National Archives*

The first few *Essex*-class aircraft carriers had lateral catapults on the hangar deck, designated H-4A catapults, intended for launching scout planes without disrupting the parking patterns of other aircraft on the hangar deck. USS *Yorktown* was one of the carriers thus equipped. One of *Yorktown*'s very early-production F6F-3s, numbered 27, is seen here in June 1943 mounted on the H-4A catapult. The tailwheel is resting on the catapult outrigger, which was hinged to swing up and out of the way when not in use. *National Archives*

Crewmen of an unidentified aircraft carrier are conducting calisthenics on the flight deck, with two F6F-3 Hellcats, numbered 1 and 29, parked among them. The plane to the left has a cover over its canopy and windscreen, while the one to the right has the cover over the canopy. Both planes have the red border around the national insignia, which was authorized from June 28 to August 14, 1943, so this photo probably dates to July or August of that year.
National Archives

Two Grumman F6F-3 Hellcats are poised on the flight deck of USS *Yorktown* in October 1943. Although it is barely visible, there is a small, black number "00" below the horizontal stabilizer of the Hellcat to the left, signifying it was assigned to the commander of the air group (CAG). *National Archives*

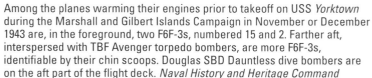

Among the planes warming their engines prior to takeoff on USS *Yorktown* during the Marshall and Gilbert Islands Campaign in November or December 1943 are, in the foreground, two F6F-3s, numbered 15 and 2. Farther aft, interspersed with TBF Avenger torpedo bombers, are more F6F-3s, identifiable by their chin scoops. Douglas SBD Dauntless dive bombers are on the aft part of the flight deck. *Naval History and Heritage Command*

Crewmen are hosing down the remnants of a fire on the flight deck of USS *Enterprise* after an F6F-3, aircraft number 30, flown by Ens. Byron Johnson, crashed upon landing on November 10, 1943. Lt. Walter L. Chewning Jr. braved the flames to rescue Ens. Johnson from the cockpit. Shortly thereafter, the crewmen would push the Hellcat over the side. *Naval History and Heritage Command*

An F6F-3 from VF-1 taxis on the flight deck of USS *Yorktown* prior to taking off on a mission during 1944. Visible on the vertical fin is the Bureau Number, 41890, and the last three digits of that number are roughly painted on the cowling. The aircraft number, 9, is stenciled on the right wing and the fuselage, and the letter *K* is on the rudder. The diagonal stripe of the *Yorktown*'s air group is on the vertical fin. *National Museum of Naval Aviation*

Tightly parked Grumman F6F-3 Hellcats on an unidentified aircraft carrier are running up their engines in the foreground, preparing for another combat mission in the Pacific theater around 1943 or 1944. These Hellcats have their aircraft numbers in large figures on the fuselages, and in small figures on the landing-gear doors, the fronts of the cowlings, and, interestingly, on the upper parts of the vertical fins. To the rear of the flight deck are Douglas SBD Dauntless dive bombers; these aircraft were supplanted on aircraft carriers by Curtiss SB2C Helldivers in 1944. *National Museum of Naval Aviation*

Crewmen stand by while a plane director signals the pilot of a just-landed F6F-3 forward on the flight deck of USS *Lexington* (CV-16) sometime between late 1943 and 1944. The Hellcat's aircraft number, 26, is on the front of the cowling and the main landing-gear doors. *Naval History and Heritage Command*

Flames are snapping around the wreckage of an F6F-3 Hellcat that crashed on takeoff from Ondonga Air Strip on New Georgia in the Solomon Islands on December 10, 1943. To the right is the top of the right wing, while the severed rear of the fuselage and empennage is upside down to the left. *Naval History and Heritage Command*

Fighter pilots on USS *Lexington* (CV-16) have just received orders to man their planes. The Hellcat in the foreground is F6F-3, BuNo 66197, and the aircraft number is 38. The US Navy officially released this photograph on January 23, 1945, so the photo predates that. *Naval History and Heritage Command*

A tractor is respotting an F6F-3 on the flight deck of the light aircraft carrier USS *Monterey* (CVL-26) during operations in the Central Pacific toward the end of 1943. At intervals alongside the teak planks of the deck are metal tie-down strips, for attaching rope stays for securing aircraft. *Naval History and Heritage Command*

Airedales are servicing two F6F-5s on an unidentified aircraft carrier. The corrugated surface of the interior of the gun bay door is visible on the wing of the Hellcat to the right; this surface is painted blue, which is possibly the same glossy Dark Sea Blue used on the exterior of the aircraft. *National Archives*

Grumman F6F-3 Hellcats are lined up on a tarmac at an unidentified naval air station around 1943–44. They are equipped with Mk. 2 150-gallon drop tanks. At least the first two planes have the bottom cowl flaps; the bullet-shaped fairing on the cowling to the front of the side exhausts was a characteristic of the first 1,500 F6F-3s. *Naval History and Heritage Command*

Grumman F6F-3 Hellcats from Fighting Squadron 10, commanded by Lt. Cdr. William R. "Killer" Kane, are returning to USS *Enterprise* (CV-6) after the first day of strikes on Truk Lagoon in the Caroline Islands on February 16, 1944. The pilot of the nearest plane has initiated the folding of the wings and is moving forward on the flight deck to make room for more returning planes.
National Archives

An F6F-3 from VF-2 "Rippers" has just launched from the hangar-deck catapult of USS *Hornet* (CV-12) on February 25, 1944. The plane number is 21, and on the fuselage to the front of the windscreen is a round marking, likely the squadron's insignia.
Tailhook Association

Crewmen of the USS *Hornet* (CV-12) are working on a mix of aircraft types following the Marianas Campaign in June 1944. During that month, aircraft from that carrier, including Hellcats, had participated in the massive slaughter of Japanese airplanes called the Marianas Turkey Shoot. In the foreground of this photo, parked to the starboard of several Helldivers and Avengers, are two Grumman F6F-3s: one numbered 18 and another numbered 23. *National Archives*

In an undated view from the superstructure of USS *Essex*, looking through several signal flags, F6F-3 Hellcats of VF-15 prepare for a mission. The closest plane is the "Minsi," assigned to Capt. David McCampbell, who would become the top-scoring US Navy ace of World War II. This was the first of three Hellcats McCampbell would fly, named the "Minsi," "Minsi II," and "Minsi III." The latter two were F6F-5s. Marked on the doors of the main landing gear are "A.G.C.," standing for air group commander; McCampbell became commander of Air Group 15 in February 1944. His use of the "Minsi" evidently was brief, spanning May to June 1944. *Naval History and Heritage Command*

In an undated view from the bridge of USS *Essex* (CV-9), looking out over the two forward twin 5-inch/38-caliber gun mounts, F6F-5 Hellcats from the renowned Fighting Squadron 15 (VF-15) are spotted on the forward part of the flight deck. Commanded by Capt. David McCampbell, this squadron was a prominent participant in the Marianas Turkey Shoot, June 19–20, 1944. *Naval History and Heritage Command*

At 1717 on July 1, 1944, during a landing on USS *Ticonderoga* (CV-14) during the carrier's shakedown cruise off Trinidad, Ens. J. G. Fraifogl, US Navy Reserve, had just landed his F6F-5, numbered 4, when the shock of the landing jarred a drop tank loose. The propeller slashed the tank, visible to the right, and it was seeping fuel and smoke when this photo was taken. An instant later, it burst into fire, threatening to engulf the flight deck and the aircraft, but alert firefighters quickly doused the flames. The pilot escaped, but the Hellcat was badly damaged. Note the two support straps for the drop tank, still dangling from the belly. *Naval History and Heritage Command*

Two F6F-3N night fighters from Marine Night Fighter Squadron 534 (VMF[N]-534), Marine Air Group 21 (MAG-21), taxi on the runway at the recently captured Orote Field, Guam, on August 4, 1944. These planes were painted in standard tricolor camouflage. To the right is another Hellcat, possibly an F6F-3N, pointed in the opposite direction. *National Archives*

Wreckage of a twin-engine Mitsubishi bomber is in the right background of this view of an F6F-3N night fighter parked on Orote Field, Guam, on August 4, 1944. This was one of the first US airplanes to land on the newly repaired and reconditioned airfield. *National Archives*

A VMF(N)-534 Grumman F6F-3N, aircraft number 10, radome visible on the right wing, warms its engine at Orote Field, Guam, late in the afternoon of August 21, 1944. The plane served with VMF[N]-534), Marine Air Group 21 (MAG-21). On the cowling is the squadron's insignia: a dark-blue triangle edged in gold, with a yellow crescent moon and a blue cat with white gloves on a cloud, wearing a black top hat and holding a Tommy gun. Two other Hellcats are in the background. *Naval History and Heritage Command*

Grumman F6F-3 Hellcats from VF-8 are warming their engines preparatory to launching from USS *Bunker Hill* (CV-17) on October 27, 1944. On the vertical tails, above and below the aircraft numbers, are the horizontal white bars that signified the *Bunker Hill*'s air group. The planes are painted in tricolor camouflage. *Naval History and Heritage Command*

Sailors are swabbing the flight deck of USS *Hancock* (CV-19) on November 3, 1944, during the invasion of the Philippines. Adjacent to them is an F6F-5 numbered 32; the windscreen that was particular to that model is partially visible. *National Archives*

Grumman Hellcats from VF-15 are lining up for takeoff from USS *Essex* (CV-9), part of Task Group 38.3, off the Philippine Islands on November 5, 1944. At that time, the *Essex* had ten F6F-5s, serving with VB-15; thirty-eight F6F-3s, serving with VF-15; and two F6F-3Ps, with VF-15. These planes appear to have the windscreens of F6F-5s. *National Archives*

A pilotless F6F-5, BuNo 70328, and aircraft number 17, from VF-7 is secured to a catapult on USS *Hancock* on November 6, 1944. The nickname "Ripper" is painted in script below the windscreen, next to the squadron insignia: a pentagon with a horseshoe and blunderbuss. On the vertical tail is the squadron's lucky-horseshoe symbol. Aft of the pilot's head armor are the two small, fixed windows that remained until partway through F6F-5 production. *National Archives*

A Hellcat, numbered 88, has been secured in advance of a storm on Falalop Island, Ulithi Atoll, Caroline Islands, on November 8, 1944. The plane has been tied down, the wheels chocked with sandbags, and covers are over the cowling and the wing-fold joint. *National Archives*

Crewmen scramble to assist the pilot and secure an F6F-5, plane number 90 of VF-30, which has just suffered landing-gear failure during an arrested landing on USS *Enterprise* (CV-6) on November 9, 1944. The pilot, Lt. (j.g.) Mahlon D. Cooley, survived the accident without injuries, and the Hellcat was not seriously damaged. *National Archives*

In the second of a series of photos of the crash of Mahlon D. Cooley's F6F-5 on USS *Enterprise*, many more deck crewmen have gathered around the plane, including firefighters. A tractor-towed crash-and-salvage crane is being positioned to recover the Hellcat. *National Archives*

In the third and final photo in a series documenting the crash of Lt. Cooley's F6F-5 on USS *Enterprise,* the crash-and-salvage crane has been positioned to the right front of the aircraft. With the assistance of the crane, the Hellcat will be moved out of the way quickly so operations can resume on the flight deck.
National Archives

Grumman F6F-3N night fighter, BuNo 43036, has just experienced a rather violent landing on the light carrier USS *Bataan* (CVL-29) on November 21, 1944. The arrestor hook had caught a wire, but the right wing struck a barrier wire, demolishing the radome. Note the unusual position of the aircraft number, 18, on the side of the turtle deck aft of the cockpit.
National Archives

An F6F-3N night fighter, number 338, has lost control during a landing on the escort carrier USS *Kasaan Bay* (CVE-69) on November 28, 1944, and, propeller still spinning, the aircraft appears to be on the verge of going over the side. The left wing is not far from one of the carrier's smokestacks.
National Archives

The original label for this photo is vague, stating that it shows a Hellcat after "crash landing" on a light carrier, either USS *Monterey* (CVL-26) or USS *Cowpens* (CVL-25), during the Gilbert and Marshall Islands operations in November and December 1943. However, a comparison of this photo with a sizable series of images taken during and after an incident in which F6F-3, BuNo 66101, aircraft number 3 of VF-25, landed while on fire on the *Cowpens* (CV-25) indicates that this photo shows that plane after the fire was extinguished but before the irreparably damaged Hellcat was pushed off the flight deck. The pilot, Lt. (j.g.) Alfred W. Magee Jr., USNR, was not injured. *Naval History and Heritage Command*

The next several photos document flight deck operations either on USS *Cowpens* (CVL-25) or USS *Monterey* (CVL-26) during the Gilbert and Marshall Islands operations in November or December 1943. It seems more likely that the ship was the *Cowpens*, given the known presence of a photographer with color film on that carrier during that time. Here, F3F-3s are being readied for takeoff on a combat mission. To the right is aircraft number 12, to the left of which is number 1. *Naval History and Heritage Command*

The first two F6F-3s on the right are warming their engines. Wheels are chocked until the planes are ready to move forward on the deck. In the left foreground is another F6F-3, with a row of Avenger torpedo bombers to its rear. *Naval History and Heritage Command*

While Avenger pilots to the left prepare to start their engines, two F6F-3 Hellcats parked diagonally to the right of the photo are warming their engines. These are numbered 2 (*left*) and 10 (*right*). Farther aft on the flight deck are parked more Hellcats. *Naval History and Heritage Command*

In the hall where the US Navy held its Sixth War Loan Exhibition, in Chicago, Illinois, in December 1944, in the foreground is a factory-fresh F6F-5 Hellcat. The focus of this exhibition was the urgency of winning the war in the Pacific theater. *National Archives*

At an unidentified airfield in the Marianas Islands on December 15, 1944, Marine mechanics are performing maintenance on the R-2800 engine of a Grumman F6F-3N night fighter assigned to a squadron in the Fourth Marine Aircraft Wing. The Hellcat night fighters were executing their first combat missions within a few days of the capture of this airfield. *National Archives*

Two mechanics, including one at the top identified as Aviation Machinist's Mate 1st Class Brannam, of VF-16, are working on an R-2800 engine in an F6F-3 Hellcat during a break between airstrikes on Kwajalein and Mili around early December 1943. *National Archives*

An F6F-5, or possibly a night fighter version of that model, considering the dull, almost black appearance of the paint on the cowling, is undergoing engine maintenance at an unidentified base around late 1944. To the right, a mechanic is selecting an implement in a drawer in a tool cart.
National Archives

Plane handlers are steadying the folded right wing of an F6F-5 Hellcat on a deck-edge elevator on an unidentified aircraft carrier. The date is unknown: F6F-5s began entering service in mid-1944, and the photo has a Navy filing date of May 24, 1945. Note the contrast between the dull paint finish on the cowling and the folded wing, versus the gloss finish on the tail, including the reflection of the number "48" on the horizontal stabilizer. *Naval History and Heritage Command*

Armorers are loading 5-inch high-velocity aerial rockets (HVARs) onto zero-length launchers on the right wing of an F6F-5 numbered 32 on an unidentified aircraft carrier before a raid against Japanese naval forces in Manila Bay sometime between September 1944 and early January 1945. The man next to the cowling is handing a fuel hose up to the man on the wing. *Naval History and Heritage Command*

A Hellcat with an F6F-5-type windscreen, aircraft number 5, is about to take off from the light aircraft carrier USS *Independence* (CVL-22) around late 1944. In the foreground, an airedale kneels by the left wheel of another Hellcat with its engine running. In the right background is a crane.
Naval History and Heritage Command

A Hellcat that has just landed on USS *Enterprise* (CV-6) has suffered a broken propeller blade; it is the right-hand blade in this photo. On each side of the plane aft of the wings is a firefighter in a protective suit. *National Archives*

The pilot of the same Hellcat seen in the preceding photo is easing himself out of the cockpit after landing on the *Enterprise* (CV-6) in the Pacific around May 1945. A tractor has arrived to tow the disabled plane. *National Archives*

This elevated view of hundreds of F6F Hellcats tightly arranged, with wings folded, inside Hangar 2 at the Aircraft Storage Depot, NAS Santa Ana, California, in February 1945 is testament to the impressive production capacity of Grumman during World War II. Grumman completed 4,402 F6F-3s of all types and 7,868 F6F-5s. *Naval History and Heritage Command*

Soon after the conclusion of World War II, a number of F6F-3 Hellcats were converted to F6F-3K unmanned, remotely controlled drones. This example, numbered 11, was photographed at NAS Atlantic City, New Jersey, on March 13, 1946. It was one of several F6F-3Ks detailed to participate in the Operations Crossroads nuclear tests at Bikini Atoll in the Pacific in July of that year. *Naval History and Heritage Command*

Six tails of the F6F-3K drones assembled at NAS Atlantic City are painted, *left to right*, pink, yellow, dark blue, blue-gray, and red. The last plane in line, painted a dark blue or possibly black, shares the same aircraft number as the second one in line, 11. The next photo reveals that that Hellcat was painted overall in that dark color, and not in the same red paint as the drone airplanes; thus, the dark-colored plane may have been a manned Hellcat. *National Museum of Naval Aviation*

At least eleven F6F-3K drones are visible in this photo taken at NAS Atlantic City on March 13, 1946. The empennage and aft part of the fuselage of each plane destined for use in Operation Crossroads was painted in a color associated with that aircraft's remote-control radio frequency. Tail colors that are visible include white, red, yellow, pink, and green. Individual aircraft numbers were painted on the tails and cowlings. *Naval History and Heritage Command*

The same line of Operation Crossroads F6F-3Ks (and possibly a manned Hellcat at the far end of the line) at NAS Atlantic City is viewed from the left front. The first F6F-3K has the nickname "JANIE" painted in white below the number "14" on the cowling; this Hellcat, BuNo 41834, survives and is currently displayed in replica tricolor camouflage at the Steven F. Udvar-Hazy Center, National Air and Space Museum. *National Museum of Naval Aviation*

Grumman F6F-3K, aircraft number 2, from the Operation Crossroads drones, is observed from the left rear, showing the cross-shaped antenna on the top of the vertical fin and the connected wire antennas. The F6F-3Ks employed in Operation Crossroads were to collect air samples and data on radioactivity following the detonation of the atomic devices at Bikini Atoll in July 1946. *National Museum of Naval Aviation*

Navy ground crewmen are securing a Grumman F6F-3K drone, which has just returned from the seventh in a series of seven flights during the Operation Crossroads atomic-bomb tests at Bikini Atoll, to collect samples from the radioactive clouds. In the foreground, technicians are handling special boxes that had been mounted under the wings for the tests. These boxes contained a treated paper for collecting the samples. *Naval History and Heritage Command*

An airedale is adjusting the holdback at the rear of an F6F-5 being prepared for a catapult launch from USS *Wright* (CVL-49) around 1949. The "C" tail code was that of US Naval Reserve aircraft based at NAS Columbus, Ohio. During this period, Navy Reserve aircraft wore an International Orange band around the aft fuselage, and that feature is present here. *National Museum of Naval Aviation*

Pilots, officers, and deck crewmen are gathered around two tractors on the flight deck of a light aircraft carrier, probably USS *Wright* (details of the superstructure of the *Wright* closely match those seen in this photo). In the background are several F6F-5s from NAS Columbus, Ohio, with the "C" tail code. *National Museum of Naval Aviation*

After World War II, the Navy's fleet of F6Fs was dispersed, with some serving as training aircraft at Navy bases, others being assigned to the US Naval Air Reserve, and still others being placed in "mothballs"—long-term storage. In this photo, in a blimp hangar at NAS Santa Ana, California, on August 23, 1948, a group of mothballed Grumman F6F-5s and Vought F4U Corsairs in the background are being prepared for reactivation. *Tailhook Association*

In the 1950s, the Naval Air Reserve and Navy training squadrons continued to fly F6F Hellcats, although in ever-dwindling numbers. Here, several Hellcats are being taken out of mothballs for reactivation at Litchfield Park, Arizona, in March 1950. The plane in the foreground, armed with a 20 mm cannon in the wing, may have been an F6F-5N or one of the limited number of F6F-5s armed with the mix of two 20 mm cannons and two .50-caliber machine guns. *National Archives*

An F6F-5 has just landed on the light aircraft carrier USS *Cabot* (CVL-28) during a Naval Air Reserve carrier qualification exercise out of Pensacola, Florida, sometime in the period between August 1950 and mid-1952. *National Museum of Naval Aviation*

In a companion image to the preceding one, an F6F-5 has just landed on the *Cabot*, and plane handlers are sprinting out to move the Hellcat farther forward on the flight deck. In the foreground is a crash-and-salvage crane, to the rear of which several crewmen are starting up a tractor. The man running to the right of the tractor is pulling a tow bar, for the use of the tractor in pulling the aircraft along the deck. *National Museum of Naval Aviation*

An F6F-5 Hellcat on the flight deck of the light carrier USS *Cabot* wears a "CB" tail code. This code was used for Carrier Qualification Training Unit 4 (CQTU-4) from August 1950 to mid-1952, and several photos exist of Hellcats in these markings landing or taking off from the *Cabot* in this specific period.
National Museum of Naval Aviation